101 QUESTIONS
ANSWERED ABOUT SPIRIT

PATRICIA STERRY

First published 1996 by Patricia Sterry, 44 St Mark Street, Gloucester GL1 2QQ

© Copyright 1996 Patricia Sterry

ISBN 0 9528940 0 9

All rights reserved. No part of this publication may be reproduced, stored in a retrieval system, or transmitted in any form or by any means, electronic, mechanical, photocopying, recording or otherwise, without the prior permission of the publisher.

Designed by Martin Latham
Edited by Fiona Latham
Cover illustration by Sarah Dalton

Printed by Q Print, Bonds Mill, Stonehouse, Glos.

INTRODUCTION

Where do I start with an introduction to Spirit, when there is no start, no middle or no end, no rules and regulations – just knowledge and understanding that we are all in some way striving for (even if we do not realise it)? The 101 questions that I have answered in this book are the ones that I have been asked time and time again during my years of being a medium and healer. My grandparents were spiritualists which meant that although I didn't understand Spirit, I was brought up with the knowledge that they were always around and ready to help.

I have answered these questions with my understanding of things: therefore it is for you in your heart to judge whether this understanding sits right with you. Some of you will read this book and not agree with a word, and I would say to you that that's fine because where you stand on your pathway is right for you. Some of you will read this book and feel as if you have had pieces of a puzzle put into place for you. That's fine too. If only one sentence of this book makes you think differently about yourself or what's around you then my job is done.

Without the help of my family and friends who have made this book a reality my task could not have been completed. Without my Spirit friends and guides this book would not even have been a thought. It took a great deal of persuasion on their part to even get me to start this book and it has taken a great deal of their prompting and effort to get me to finish it. Now that we have, I pray with all my heart that the words contained in these pages will help you in some way to find out about you, your helpers and your unique pathway.

1. What is Spirit?

The first question is the easiest of the 101 questions to answer, because the answer is that we are. We are part of Spirit and Spirit are part of us. Whilst we are here on this earth plane our Spirits are encased in our cumbersome bodies. When we pass to the Spirit world our Spirits are free to have total understanding again. Once we have passed we go into light, love and harmony, and we become like balls of light. When Spirit present themselves to us they do so as they were when they were last on this earth plane, but they only do this for recognition.

2. Where do our individual Spirits come from?

We are all in the beginning part of God the Source, and we fragment off and become an individual Spirit with our own light. This light grows with our knowledge and understanding.

3. Where are Spirit?

Very often when we talk of Spirit we talk about them being upstairs and look upwards as if towards heaven, but they are in fact all around us, in front of us and behind us. We can't see them because they are in a different dimension to our own. I can explain this by saying it's as though we have an invisible world going on around us that we are not aware of. Most of the time this adjacent world does not affect our own – this is because the next world is made up of light and energy and not any solid form. When we see, sense or hear Spirit just for a moment it is as though we have opened a doorway between our two worlds. We call the next world "Spirit Dimension".

4. Can our Spirit die?

I personally don't believe that our Spirit can die. It can get stuck, and it can go to different levels, but I do believe it always exists.

5. Why are Spirit with us?

Spirit are with us because they choose to be. When a Spirit passes over it has choices to make about what it wishes to do next. It can choose to stay around loved ones that it has left here on the earth plane until it's their time to pass; it can choose to go to a different level to learn more for its progression; or it can choose to come back to earth to learn a lesson or lessons it hasn't done in its previous life. It can also choose to stay where it passes and not progress to the light. There are many more choices than these, a lot of which are quite complicated to understand, so I have only listed a few. If a Spirit chooses to stay around loved ones it stays to give help and support through its loved one's lifetime.

6. Can Spirit hear and see everything that we do?

Spirit do not see or hear us in the physical sense of these words. Spirit see us as our light and hear our thoughts. Most mediums have conversations mind to mind with Spirit. Spirit do not see the very practical side of our lives such as going to the loo, they see only our light.

7. What is the difference between a Ghost and a Spirit?

We in our human form are made up of mind, body and spirit (see Question 75). About half an inch from the outside of our physical body we have what we term an etheric body, which is an exact copy of our physical body and is mostly invisible to the naked eye. When we pass to Spirit our etheric body should disintegrate. However if we pass very quickly or in trauma the etheric body remains intact whilst the Spirit passes on. It may take hundreds of years for the etheric body to disintegrate, which is why people talk of seeing ghosts in period costumes such as "Grey Ladies", "Headless Horsemen" etc. As a medium I have been asked many times to go and sort out a "ghost" which in fact is impossible to do because as the Spirit has already passed there is no one to communicate with.

8. Is working with Spirit the same as working with witchcraft?

Working with Spirit is very different from working with witchcraft. When we work with Spirit we link up to the light and the God energy. Witchcraft works on the magnetic forces of the earth. Used positively by White Witches these forces can do a great deal of good. But used with the negativity around us they can be quite destructive.

9. What about God?

Of all the 101 questions in this book, for me this is the most important one to answer and if someone had asked me about six or seven years ago I would not have been able to answer it. Everyone's interpretation of God is different and in my opinion *should* be different. I can only give you my own personal view which is that God is the light or the source, whichever word you wish to use and not a judgemental character who sits on a throne waiting to tell us whether we will go up or down! I had God described to me once as the back of a comb and us as all the teeth attached to the back of the comb. Even if we feel we come adrift we cannot get lost because in our hearts we are all part of the source or the light. Through this life most of us are conditioned not to see the best in ourselves, and only seeing the worst in ourselves dulls our lights, but nothing or no one can truly extinguish our light.

10. What about Jesus?

Having started life as a spiritualist I'd never really believed in or even thought about Jesus and never really thought that he had walked the earth plane. But through what I have learnt, friends, I now totally believe that Jesus did walk our earth plane and was a great healer and prophet and that the word he gave was love of our fellow humans and light within our own hearts. The most important thing that I believe he tried to teach was that we are all as important as one another and on a Spiritual level we all have as much to learn as one another. There are many people now who work with Spirit who actually see Jesus clairvoyantly and I do believe he comes now at this time in our lives to bring us back to his teachings, which are the love of one another and respect for ourselves.

11. Is there a devil?

Again I can only answer this question in my own beliefs and that is that there is no such thing as a figure with a forked tail and horns as we are conditioned to believe in. Of course as well as light and positivity there will always be darkness and negativity, but in my opinion it is not personified by a traditional devil.

12. Is there a hell?

In my own personal belief hell is not a place of fire and brimstone. But hell can be choosing to come back here to earth to do it all again to learn more lessons and to add to our store of knowledge.

13. Do we all go to heaven?

If you think of the next dimension as being heaven then yes, there is a heaven and we can choose whether or not we walk there, but we all do have the opportunity to go on and progress.

14. Does God or Spirit judge us?

Neither God nor Spirit judge us. The only ones that judge us are ourselves. How many times have you heard of people who have had near-death experiences tell of seeing their lives pass before them, seeing what they have achieved and not achieved? I firmly believe that we are the ones who look at the life we have just experienced and decide what we do with the achievements and the failings of that life.

15. Do Spirit have a sense of humour?

In my experience some Spirit do have a great sense of humour. I have always maintained that to walk my pathway with me my guides have needed a sense of humour. In fact I have a North American Indian guide who has a terrific sense of humour, although there are also very serious guides that never seem to crack a smile. I have a great belief that if a guide had a sense of humour in their last incarnation it does stay with them.

16. Are all people that work with Spirit good people?

In every single profession there are those who dedicate themselves to the work they do and those who do not. Some people, if they are not trained properly, can tap into mischievous Spirit and work on the negative side. This is why if you wish to go and see someone who works with Spirit you should always go to see someone who comes highly recommended. Those of us that dedicate our lives to working with Spirit would be the first to say that just because we work with Spirit it doesn't make us special or different from anyone else. Believe me, I for one make huge mistakes in my life, but I do strive to learn from them.

17. Is there bad Spirit?

If a Spirit is stuck (see Question 19) it can take on earthly negativity. In our world at this moment of time there is a lot of negativity, with people being short of money and not trusting one another. A stuck Spirit can absorb this negativity and it can become mischievous and angry, but it usually can be talked to and reasoned with and more often that not it can be helped over to the light.

18. Can bad Spirit come through?

As I have explained trapped Spirit can take on negativity and be mischievous which is why we have training to make sure that we are only bringing light Spirit through and that we are able to feel any negative Spirit around. We learn to always ask for protection and this is why no one should play or mess around with contacting Spirit unless they have had proper training.

19. Why do Spirit get stuck?

Sometimes Spirit choose to stay where they pass. This is termed being stuck. You may ask why a Spirit would choose to be stuck. It may be that the Spirit that has passed is too afraid to go into the light. Sometimes they are afraid because they are not sure where they are going, or it may be simply that they are not ready to go to the light so they stay in a kind of limbo between the two dimensions. I will say, however, that it is my experience that a stuck Spirit will usually decide to go to the light sooner or later. When that decision is made then it takes help from both sides of the dimension. We hold what is called a rescue circle, where we join with those from Spirit to create an opening between the dimensions which then allows the stuck Spirit to pass through and be taken for healing.

20. If Spirit know all the answers why don't they tell us?

Spirit may know all the answers to our lives but we do have such a thing as free will, which means that we have to make our own decisions, and Spirit are not allowed to interfere. If we ask for help they will do their best to help us, but it is important to realise that unless we actually ask for help Spirit are not allowed to interfere.

21. Do Spirit get frustrated with us?

Spirit do not get frustrated with us. They understand that we are human and that by doing a task over and over again we do eventually learn the lesson of the task. We must always remember that Spirit don't have the sense of waiting that we do so therefore they don't have the sense of frustration that we do.

22. Does working with Spirit hold them back?

Working with Spirit holds neither them nor us back – as I have explained earlier, if Spirit stay with us it is because they choose to. As much as we can learn from them they can learn from us. When most of them were last on the earth plane it may have been centuries ago when obviously things were very different. Being with us they can see the way that we deal with situations and they can gain knowledge from our experiences. Being able to learn from one another means that both sides of the dimension can grow in understanding and wisdom.

23. Is there any time in Spirit?

Quite simply the answer to this question is NO. Spirit knows no time – our lifetimes to them are like the blink of an eye. They find it quite hard to comprehend that we live our lives by the ticking of a clock.

24. What are guides?

Guides are Spirit that have walked the earth plane many times and have learnt all the earthly lessons that there are. We all have guides that walk our lives with us, and they present themselves to us in the form that they last walked the earth plane. They might appear as a monk or nun, for example, or they might have been somebody quite ordinary – a friend of mine has a guide who always wears a pin-stripe suit and bowler hat!

"Guardian angels" are the same thing as guides. For some people the concept of angels is easier to accept and that is why Spirit may sometimes show themselves in this form and why, therefore, there are reported sightings of angels.

Guides are wise Spirit and will freely give any parts of their wisdom if asked. They do however also learn from us. In many cases it has been hundreds of years since a guide has walked the earth plane and it is through our eyes they are able to see the progression on earth through the ages.

25. Why are our guides with us?

Our guides are with us because they choose to be. They are there to help us through our pathways and to give guidance, NOT TO MAKE OUR DECISIONS FOR US. My belief is that we have more than one guide and that at different times of our lives and in facing different problems a guide will step in who can help us deal with those problems. For example, if someone is totally stressed and worked up very often there will be a nun or monk to bring peace to them through the stress, to calm the mind and to focus it, therefore bringing an ability to see the problem more clearly. I also do believe that our very strong guides have been a part of our past lives and that they may have been with us either physically or spiritually in many of those lives.

26. Why are so many guides American Indians?

A lot of famous guides have been American Indians in their last lives. American Indians have great knowledge of Mother Earth and Spirit. They respect the animal kingdom, the plant kingdom, the sea kingdom, etc. and before they take anything from Mother Earth they ask her permission and honour her. They have endured great hardship with joy in the knowledge that it is part of their growth and progression. I was amazed when I went to a lecture given by a North American Indian to find that native Americans do not believe in guides at all. When I asked Spirit about this they told me that the native Indians do not need guides as the life they are born into is one where there is a total belief in "The Great Spirit" (God) and they need no help to reach the source. Most of us are born into very dogmatic religions where we have fear and are not taught that we can actually communicate with the source, and therefore we do need guidance to reach that understanding. Who better than those who lived on the earth plane with that knowledge?

27. Does everyone who believes in Spirit go to the Spiritualist Church?

No! Not everyone who believes in Spirit goes to the Spiritualist Church. There are many now that believe that they have no religion but believe in God as the source or the light, and believe that you can talk to God anywhere, not just in a building, no matter what faith it contains. I myself do believe that Spiritualist Churches are some of the most peaceful places that there are and that they are a good first step for people who have no knowledge of Spirit. In the Spiritualist Church there is a lot of good philosophy that is brought through and some of the evidence of life after death brought through in the Church can be quite startling.

28. What happens in a Spiritualist Church?

There are generally two types of service that go on in a Spiritualist Church. The Sunday service consists of hymns, opening prayers, and healing prayers and thoughts sent to those who are sick and the suffering in our world. Then there is a reading which some mediums will have written themselves, or one from an inspirational book. Then there is an address where the medium will talk usually straight from Spirit giving philosophy from Spirit that may help us in our daily lives; then there is the clairvoyance where messages are brought through from the congregation's loved ones, and finally there is a hymn and closing prayer. Clairvoyance services are held on different nights depending on the church – these are where the evening is turned over to the medium to bring messages from loved ones who have passed. The healing evenings are where there are healers ready at the church to give hands-on healing to anyone that comes along. No one has to belong to the church to go along and most churches make newcomers very welcome.

29. Why do other religions think that working with Spirit is evil?

Many other religions believe that people such as mediums are evil and they hold Spirit back, or even that when we are talking to Spirit we are talking to evil Spirit. Most mediums including myself actually have a great faith and belief in God, the source or the light.

God in a lot of religions is made out to be our judge and is portrayed as a threat if we do not do as he wants. This belief puts fear into people and hangs like a threat over their heads. It is my personal belief that we judge ourselves when we pass over and in fact that when it is our time to be in the next dimension, we look at what we have achieved and not achieved in this life and then we can decide what we are going to do. I have to stress that this is my belief from what I have learnt over the time I have worked with Spirit.

I would also like to stress that I am in no way decrying other religions or putting down their beliefs because I also believe that we should all be allowed freedom of choice and whatever religion we choose to follow is the one that we need to learn from in this life. We must feel what's right for us within our own lives and not someone else's. Each of our pathways is different from the next person's so how could we say what is right or wrong for someone when we don't know what they've come back here to learn or experience?

30. Can Spirit communicate with animals?

Spirit can communicate with animals on a telepathic level. Also, as a medium I have very often experienced animals who have passed coming back to say "hello" to their owners.

31. Are animals sensitive?

Yes, all animals are sensitive but like humans some are more sensitive than others. What we as humans haven't realised is that animals also take on traumas of things that happen to them in life. Domestic animals can end up in the most loving home possible, but if they have had any kind of ill treatment that will stay with them and make them very difficult to deal with. I have done quite a bit of work with horses clearing their emotional blocks the same way as humans would be cleared and it works well. I have also found that the same system can be used for domestic animals, which also seems to be having great success.

32. Are children more sensitive to Spirit?

Definitely, children are very sensitive to Spirit. Between the ages of 0–5 years children will very often have unseen friends or talk about members of their families who have passed over. The children have no fear of them, seeing light and Spirit people as a normal part of life. We as adults are guilty of saying "Don't tell lies" or "Don't be silly", and therefore we shut them down. I have found that around the age of 5 when children start school they shut down naturally. I have watched this process with my youngest daughter. We didn't have to shut her down in any way from seeing and talking to Spirit – she did it by herself. We as "responsible" adults have to learn that children very often do know the answers even though we find it incomprehensible.

33. Why do we need protection?

There are two kinds of protection we need. When we are very sensitive we can pick up all sorts of negative vibrations from the people that we are around. All sensitive people should learn that as soon as they get out of bed in the morning they need to surround themselves in light to stop anyone else's negativity being taken on. Also when we are working with Spirit we need to protect ourselves from low level Spirit or mischievous Spirit so we surround ourselves in light and ask God for protection.

34. How do I get in touch with the Spirit with me?

I would never advocate that anyone ever get in touch with Spirit unless they have been taught how to do it properly. That means going to someone who has been well trained themselves and is dedicated to showing the joy of understanding Spirit, not using it to see what's going to happen in the future. (Although Spirirt do see our complete pathways, they would never predict the future for us because that takes away our personal choice.) What working with Spirit is really about is allowing Spirit to be near us to help us be at peace within ourselves and then to help others to do the same.

35. What happens when we pass over?

When we pass over there is always someone from Spirit waiting to help us over to the next dimension. If we choose to go on to the light with them we are taken into a time of healing. Whilst we are in this time we have an opportunity to reflect on the life we have just finished and can take time to decide what we wish to do next. If someone has passed very quickly and doesn't quite know what has happened to them their process of healing will take a little longer – also if someone has passed with an illness such as cancer, then healing is said to take a little longer. I must emphasise here that there is no hard and fast rule – the time of healing depends totally on the individual.

36. What happens when children pass over?

When children pass it is probably the most traumatic experience of anyone's life. I have been asked many times why we should have to loose children of whatever age. Friends, there are many reasons but there is not one of those reasons that could make anyone that has lost a child feel any better about it. I will explain however that any child that passes over is immediately looked after by a member of their family that has already passed. Children adjust into the world of Spirit in most cases a lot more quickly and easier than adults do. I have had instances of a child coming back to commune with their family very quickly after their passing. All children grow in Spirit, but we have to realise they grow in understanding not age.

37. What happens when babies pass over?

When babies pass they are always met by a member of the family who has already passed, and are taken into healing. This is the case no matter how they pass – whether they are miscarried, aborted or still-born, they always have a direct passage into the light to be taken care of.

I would like to point out that there is debate about what time a Spirit enters a foetus. In our western culture it is believed that the Spirit enters at the moment of conception but in such cultures as North American Indian or Aboriginal it is believed that the Spirit does not enter the foetus until the time that it moves independently (i.e. around 18–24 weeks).

38. Why are some good people taken early?

People aren't "taken" early – their passing is to do with their choice and is part of their learning. Dealing with their passing is also part of the learning process of those left behind.

The term "good" often applies to those who put themselves before others. This is a magnificent quality, but there comes a time in all of our lives where we do have to put ourselves first and think of what we need as well as everyone else's needs, or else we tire ourselves and want to shut ourselves away. We must always allow ourselves time. This is probably one of the hardest things to learn because we feel it is selfish. If we can only see that in healing ourselves we can help twice as many others than we would usually, we realise it's not selfish at all.

39. What is a medium?

A medium is a person who has developed the ability to see, hear and feel into the next dimension. Think of it as a telephone line: we're in one phone box, Spirit are in another. What a medium has done is learned to pick up the receiver and dial the right number.

40. What is a trance medium?

A trance medium is a medium who allows Spirit to come through and use their voice to give philosophy. It takes great trust in Spirit to allow them through but having experienced this kind of mediumship I know that light Spirit would not harm anyone they use as a vessel. **THIS TYPE OF MEDIUMSHIP SHOULD NEVER BE TRIED UNLESS THERE IS AN EXPERIENCED MEDIUM PRESENT.**

41. What is a psychic medium?

A psychic medium is a person who will do a reading on what he or she "feels" from you. They probably will be able to see the colours in your aura (see Questions 81–2) and be able to interpret them into how you are feeling there and then. Some psychic mediums are very accurate because they sense the person that they are reading, but this has to be done with sensitivity as a psychic medium would be able to sense if there has been a great amount of pain in a person's life and this *must always* be dealt with very carefully.

42. Why do so many mediums become ill?

Mediums used to use a great deal of their own energy when communicating with Spirit. They did this by working through the Solar Plexus Chakra (see Question 83). This chakra affects the pancreas, stomach, and spleen, and can affect the heart. When the chakra is over-used all these organs are affected adversely. These days many mediums will ground to Mother Earth and link to the God light before they start to work with Spirit. This means that none of the medium's own energy is used and therefore there is no risk of straining the organs.

43. What is clairvoyance?

Clairvoyance is French for clear-seeing – this is a term used where mediums see Spirit. Most mediums, including myself, see Spirit within their minds and when we say "we see" we are actually seeing something like a video playing within our minds. Not many mediums see Spirit physically as it takes an awful lot of energy for Spirit to manifest into a physical form.

44. What is clairaudience?

Clairaudience is French for clear-hearing – this is a term used where a medium hears Spirit. Again most mediums hear Spirit within their mind as thought. When Spirit are speaking through thought the thoughts in your mind are very different from what your own would be. The words are put together very differently in your mind and they may even seem to have a bit of a different accent to them. Obviously it takes time to be aware of the differences. It also takes trust, which can only come with training and practice.

45. What is clairsentience?

Clairsentience is French for clear-sensing – this is a term used when mediums sense Spirit around them. Actually a lot of mediums use this sense a lot – you will very often hear them say such things as "I feel there's a gentleman/lady close". Sometimes mediums will feel as if they take on some of the characteristics of the Spirit they are communicating with such as "I feel as if I have a large moustache and large hands". All of these characteristics are brought for recognition only.

46. What is psychometry?

Everything that we wear or come into contact with, such as a ring, a watch or a bracelet, will absorb some of our vibrations. Mediums are able to take these items and feel the vibration that is on them. Some mediums are so adept at psychometry that they can tell the high and low points of someone's life from the vibration on their personal items.

47. What are tarot cards?

Tarot cards are thought to date back to medieval times. Most packs consist of 78 cards: 22 Major arcana cards and 56 Minor arcana cards. Many readers don't actually use pictured tarot cards, they use ordinary playing cards. Good tarot card readers usually have a great knowledge of the deck they use and don't very often change that deck. Tarot cards are often linked with the occult, but like any other tool used in readings it is the way that the tools are used that matters. If used sensitively and with light they are fine.

48. Why do we have tarot cards?

Psychics use tarot cards as a tool or as a focus point to see into the ups and downs in someone's life. In the right, sensitive, hands tarot cards can be very useful and very accurate in helping a person see a problem they are facing from a very different angle.

49. What about fortune telling?

No good medium, card reader, palmist etc., would fortune tell by saying to someone that they must do this or that. Most of us that work with Spirit will bring out a problem then help people to see the options they have to solve that problem. Fortune telling can be very destructive – for example telling someone they or a member of their family are going to pass just causes a great deal of worry and heartache. There is a fine line between help and interference in someone's life and we should never cross that line.

50. What is palmistry?

Palmistry is a very accurate science of the hand. A well-trained palmist can tell the past of our lives by looking at the left hand and our destiny by looking at the right hand. As our lives change so do the lines on our hands – our lives quite literally can be seen in our hands.

51. What is a ouija board?

A ouija board is usually a wooden board with letters, numbers, a "yes" and "no" on it. People do also make their own which has the same effect. There is a pointer which moves to different letters and spells out words. A great many people have had some kind of experience using a ouija board, sometimes with frightening consequences. This is because the ouija board is used for a laugh or a "Party Piece". These are the wrong reasons. The board will usually link the users to low level or stuck Spirit because they have no knowledge of protection or prayer. **THIS IS VERY DANGEROUS.**

52. What is numerology?

When we are born and given our names it's not by accident – the name we are given has special significance and by adding up numbers that correspond to the letters in our name we can tell our personalities, our life paths, jobs we're suited to, our karmic lessons and debts and the ages we should be when we learn specific lessons.

53. What is our karma?

Our karma is our journey through our many lifetimes, with all that we achieve and don't achieve through those lifetimes.

54. What is a karmic lesson?

A karmic lesson is something that we have designated to come back to learn in this life.

The main lessons are:

Independence and attaining what you individually need.
Relationships with each other and learning co-operation.
Expression and the joy of living.
To learn the boundaries of our limitations.
To learn to use freedom constructively.
Balance of responsibility and the responsibility of love.
To understand and to analyse without judgement.
Material satisfaction.
Selflessness and humanitarianism.

We contract to learn all of these lessons but not usually all in one lifetime.

55. Is this the only place for lessons?

I can only answer this question with what I personally believe and that is no. There is another karmic planet on which we can live and learn lessons.

56. What is a karmic debt?

If we have chosen to learn a lesson lifetime after lifetime and we do not learn from that lesson, it becomes a debt which needs to be worked out. Very often if a person has a compulsion to do a certain thing it is either part of a debt that needs to be sorted or it is their subconscious trying to help them work out the debt that they have brought with them.

57. What could we learn from knowing our lessons, debts and pathways?

When we know for sure what our pathways are it can help us to make positive changes in our lives. When we know what our lessons and debts are we know what we are dealing with, and can then take action to learn from the debts and lessons successfully.

58. Do we have the right to choose?

We always have the right to choose. We may have come to this life with specific purpose, but whether we fulfil that purpose or not is totally our choice. God and Spirit hold nothing against us, they don't judge us on what we do or do not achieve. It is always our choice how far we go and what we do.

59. What if I choose wrongly?

I don't personally believe that we can choose wrongly. Every experience is a learning process that we have to go through, the bad choices as well as the good choices. Sometimes it may feel as if we have taken the wrong pathway, but boy aren't those choices the ones we take the most experience from! So how can they be wrong?

60. What about responsibility?

This is a most important question, because we are all responsible for our own lives, what happens to us, and what doesn't happen to us. So many times I have heard people ask "Why have Spirit done this to me?" when Spirit don't actually do anything to us – we do it to ourselves. We must take responsibility for our own actions and decisions. As soon as we realise that our lives are in our own hands and no one else's, we learn to look at things with a different perspective.

61. What is reincarnation?

Reincarnation is the belief that we don't just have one life here on this earth plane but many (it has been reputed that we actually have approximately 700 lifetimes to live through, although I have to emphasise that I can't say whether this statement is strictly true or not). The purpose of coming back to earth time and time again is to experience all experiences and emotions and also to learn how to deal with all situations, but also to learn to see others not in a judgemental way but in an understanding way. Many people have a particular fascination with a time or a place in history, or maybe a country that they are drawn to for inexplicable reasons. I do believe that these draws are past life experiences just peeping through our subconscious, as all our past life experiences are held within the subconscious mind (see Question 70).

62. What is a soul-mate?

A soul-mate is someone that we have had many lifetimes with before this one. We can have more than one soul-mate on the earth at one time which can be one of the reasons for some of us getting into a real emotional mess. If we meet someone and as soon as we look in their eyes feel as if we have known them for a lifetime, we are usually coming face to face with a soul-mate.

63. What is a circle?

Put simply a circle is where a group of people gather together and sit in a circle. A circle is used because it is the shape of constant flowing energy. The circle leader should be a very experienced medium who is able to control what is coming into the circle. The people who sit in the circle say an opening prayer and ask the God light for protection and then those from Spirit for guidance on their way. The circle sitters learn how to "tune in" and are able to see Spirit. After sitting for a while it is possible to be able to give each other comfort and "messages". This process of learning varies in time with each individual. Circles are a very good way of developing the Spirit sense.

64. Why do we have open/closed circles?

Open circles are where anyone can join in. You don't have to have a permanent place – you just go where you feel like. There is a drawback to open circles which is that the group changes constantly and people find that it is harder to develop with constant change. In closed circles you have to be invited, and you get to know an awful lot about one another and one another's problems. We have open/closed circles as a way of helping and enhancing the link we have to God and Spirit.

65. What is a physical circle?

In a physical circle objects are moved around a room. These objects are usually trumpets and other sound-making instruments. These objects are supposedly moved by Spirit energy. Over the years there have been a lot of fake physical circles which have created a lot of bad press. These days you very rarely hear of physical circles taking place as there is a belief they link into a lower level of Spirit which can cause a great many problems.

66. What is déjà vu?

When we astral travel in our sleep we travel forward within our subconscious mind to make sure that we are safe (see Question 74). This is how we can feel as if we have been in an exact position and time before, knowing that we cannot possibly have. When we experience this feeling of familiarity it is termed déjà vu.

67. What is positive thought?

Positive thought is very strong – it is where we have thoughts that are only for our good such as "It's going to be a beautiful day", "I am going to get the job", "I am a calm and collected person". Positive thought works and if we only think positive things then only positive things come. It's not easy to change from being a negative thinker into a positive thinker as most of us are conditioned from childhood to expect the worst to come, so therefore the worst does come.

68. What is negative thought?

Negative thought is also very strong – this is when we have such thoughts as "It's Monday and it's going to be a miserable day", "I am not good enough to get the job", "I'm always in confusion and never come out of it". Just as with positive thought if we only think negative thoughts then only negative things will come.

69. What is the conscious mind?

The conscious mind is the part of the mind which is our waking mind. We think everyday thoughts, we make decisions, we rationalise, we debate, we argue, we feel, all with the conscious mind.

70. What is the subconscious mind?

The subconscious mind is the part of the mind where we store all our experiences, both good and bad. These experiences are not just stored from this life but from all our other lives as well. Anything that we do without thinking is done by the subconscious mind. We drive our cars, we do repetitive work, we can do a familiar journey all with the subconscious mind. Once we have learnt to drive how many of us can say that we think about changing gear? Or think about slowing down? We do these functions automatically. What we don't realise is that we are doing these functions subconsciously and that once the subconscious has learnt a repeated function it will switch in and think automatically for us.

In this life if we have had a trauma in childhood our subconscious mind can blank it out or it can change the way the trauma seemed so that we are able cope with it. Very often if someone has a block in the subconscious they will react to a situation in adulthood as they would as a child at the age of the block. For example, if someone at 10 years old was left by a parent, in adulthood if someone they loved was going away they would react as they would if they were 10 years old, whether it be kicking and screaming or going within themselves and not being able to talk. They would not know why they were reacting this way but they would not be able to help it or stop it without dealing with the cause of the reaction. Personally I feel the limits of the subconscious mind are infinite and fascinating.

71. What is visualisation?

Visualisation is another word for imagination. Our imagination plays a very important part in being able to meditate or to communicate with Spirit. When we start to work with Spirit they use our imagination to get their messages across to us. This is why often people have difficulty working out whether a message or picture has come from Spirit or whether it has come from their own imaginations. The way to determine between the two comes only with practice and experience. In meditation, visualisation (pictures within our minds) helps us to find what we need to heal ourselves or the part of ourselves that needs healing.

72. What is meditation?

Meditation is where we are able to go from our world through into the next dimension within our minds. Meditation should only be undertaken when people have been taught how to do it properly. Meditation when done right can be a lovely way to relieve stress. It can also be used for being able to see a different perspective on a problem or situation. Sometimes in meditation we may see colours and these may be the colours we need to use to enhance our lives and to heal ourselves (see Question 82).

73. What about intuition?

We all have intuition – this shows when instinctively we know when the telephone rings who it is before picking it up, or when we think that someone is going to call in and later they do. These are just two examples of intuition which we all at one time or another have had experience of. To develop intuition is easy – just start to listen to yourself, start to notice how many times these "coincidences" happen to you, and then you will realise that you do have strong intuition.

74. What is astral travel?

Astral travel is a very complex subject. When we sleep our subconscious will release things we don't need in dreams. It will also allow us to travel out of our bodies to see, within our sleep, different places and times. This is what is termed astral travel. Astral travel can be done sometimes unwittingly but is extremely dangerous, and therefore I would not advocate anyone to willingly try and leave their body.

75. What are the mind, body and spirit?

Our mind is the subconscious and the conscious mind.
Our body is our physical body holding our organs.
Our spirit is our soul.

For us to be healthy our mind, body and spirit have to be balanced.

76. What is spiritual healing?

Spiritual healing is where a healer works on the spiritual part of a patient. Spiritual healing should not be confused with faith healing, as the patient does not need to have any particular faith in the healer. No healer actually heals, it's a matter of channelling energy through the patients' bodies allowing them to balance and heal themselves.

77. What is magnetic healing?

Magnetic healing is where a healer passes some of their own vital energy to a patient. This expands the patient's energy, giving them more ability to deal with their health problems. Very often patients will say that the healer's hands get very hot. When healers give their energies it can leave them drained so they must be very careful to re-energise themselves otherwise they can become ill.

78. What is contact healing?

In contact healing a healer will ask Spirit to draw near and channel energy through to the patient. In this type of healing no energy from the healer is used and very often the healer will feel as if they have received healing as well as the patient.

79. What is absent or distance healing?

Absent or distance healing is where healing is sent to someone or somewhere by thought, and it has been proved to be quite effective. Absent healing can be sent thousands of miles to a troubled area of the world or to someone in Australia. It works by the healing thoughts being taken by healing Spirit to wherever they are needed.

80. What is the significance of colour used by Spirit?

Colour is easily brought through by Spirit in a message as to what element someone needs in their life. When a medium is doing a reading they can sometimes see a client bathed in colour. The colour that the medium sees is the colour that the client needs, e.g. if a client has had a decision to make then green can be seen around them to bring balance to the mind to help make a decision correctly.

81. What is an aura?

Our aura surrounds the outside of our bodies, and is about an inch away from our physical bodies. Sometimes if you stare at your hands you will see an energy field that looks almost like a silver outline – this is called the magnetic aura. On top of the magnetic aura there are swirls of energy which can extend out a long way from the body, and which are different colours. The colours in our auras are very significant as they change with our moods and needs.

82. What is the significance of the colours in the aura?

Everybody's interpretation of colour is different, so this guide to colour is my own interpretation.

If there is yellow in the aura it is a sign of knowledge and learning. It may also mean that a person is in need of a lot of strength.

If there is grey in the aura it is a sign of an injury or a weak spot in the corresponding part of the physical body.

If there is black in the aura it is a sign of depression and negative thought.

If there is red in the aura it is a sign of anger, or on the positive side it can be a sign of passion.

If there is pink in the aura it can be a sign of great love or the need for love.

If there is green in the aura it is a sign of balance or the need for balance.

If there is purple in the aura it is a sign of great spirituality.

If there is blue in the aura it is a sign of healing ability or a need of healing.

If there is orange in the aura it is a sign of energy or the need of energy.

Most of the colours have more than one meaning, so it needs someone who has a sound knowledge of colour and auras to read them properly.

83. What is a chakra?

A chakra is like a spinning disc of energy which is situated about an inch or two away from our bodies. We have seven main chakras and they need to be kept clear and spinning constantly so that they can draw the right amount of energy into the body.

The Base Chakra is situated at the base of the spine in the front of the pubic bone

The Digestive Chakra is situated in front of the navel area.

The Solar Plexus Chakra is situated just below the diaphragm muscle.

The Heart Chakra is situated in the heart area.

The Throat Chakra is situated in the throat area.

The Third-Eye Chakra is situated between the eyes on the forehead.

The Crown Chakra is situated about two inches above the top of the head.

If they become blocked or sluggish then physical problems occur in the corresponding part of the body.

84. What are the colours of the chakras?

The Base Chakra is coloured red.

The Digestive Chakra is coloured orange

The Solar Plexus Chakra is coloured yellow.

The Heart Chakra is coloured green but is also sometimes interpreted as pink.

The Throat Chakra is coloured blue.

The Third-Eye Chakra is coloured indigo.

The Crown Chakra is coloured violet.

85. Are we all sensitive?

We are all sensitive to varying degrees. The only people that I feel could not be developed are selfish people. These are the people who could not put themselves to one side long enough to feel someone else's pain. Being sensitive and being psychic are two very different things.

86. Can we all learn to be sensitive?

Everyone is sensitive but anyone who wants to work hard, and is willing to clear out all their old rubbish and see things in a very different way can develop their sensitivity much more.

87. Why can't I feel my mother/father?

Many people who have lost parents they were very close to ask me this question. They want so much to feel their loved one by them, or they even want to be able to see that loved one physically, but they simply try too hard. On most occasions I find that the loved one is there around them all the time, they just block out being able to feel them. Often, however, they say, "I smelt their perfume or aftershave but I thought it was my imagination." Smell is one of the easiest tools for Spirit to use so don't take smells as coincidence when they come out of the blue.

Personally I lost my father to Spirit some twenty years ago now. I never saw him or felt him and thought that he had deserted me. As you can imagine I was quite upset with him so I unwittingly blocked him out even more. I was quite poorly in April 1994 and whilst in hospital saw him clearly standing at the end of my bed and knew then that he was there for me and always had been: I just hadn't believed it. Since that time on occasions I do see him but I know now that he is always there for me.

88. How do I develop?

Development can only be done with care. I do believe almost everyone can be developed to one level or another, so again if you wish to develop intuition, or want to work with Spirit, go to someone who has had past spiritual teaching experience and find out about their reputation before joining or committing yourself to any group. Someone that works properly certainly would not mind being asked some questions or allowing you to "sit in" or explaining exactly what happens in a group before you joined. Just because there are titles such as "medium" or "healer" do not think that we are above you. We're not – all of us are still learning to a great degree. Mediums, healers and teachers are people that have very often been through just as much rubbish as the next person. We are all special, not just those who have titles.

89. Why do we have such hard lives?

Simply, we have hard lives because we choose them and because we're supposed to learn from them. When we are in Spirit waiting to come back to the earth plane we choose our pathway and the experiences of that pathway. Believe me, personally I used to think that the theory that we choose our pathways was one of the hardest things to accept ever, but I have realised that everything that is gone through in life has the ability to teach us how to deal with things and then to let them go. In letting go, we can move on and help many others who are going through the same experience with a non-judgemental view.

90. Why me!

We all go around in life saying "Why me?", but we must realise that we go through every experience for a reason and that each crisis has great learning potential in it. Then maybe we realise that if we take the lesson and learn what we need from it, we would not have to keep going through the same experience time after time. So instead of saying "Why me?" say, "OK, maybe I did not like that experience but I have learnt from it and I don't need to go through it again".

91. Why do we have free will?

We have free will so that we can learn from lessons, have our own joys and heartaches and go from one experience to another. We have free will to say yes or no as we wish to. If we did not have free will we would all be like computers waiting for the next command to be fed in. We may think it would be easier for someone else to make our decisions for us, but how many of us would really like it? We are free spirits, each with an inbuilt knowledge of what is wrong and what is right for us individually. If we do something that we know to be wrong we do so with our own free will, therefore it must follow that we are also willing to take the consequences of our actions. By having our own pathways, no matter how difficult, our destinies can lie completely in our own hands.

92. Do we have set pathways?

I do believe that when we are in Spirit waiting to come back to the earth plane we do choose pathways, what to learn and what we wish to achieve. Many of us go for years feeling very discontented no matter what we take on, then out of the blue comes an opportunity to change direction and if we take it we feel "This is it, this is what I'm meant to be doing". This is what's meant by coming onto a set or destined pathway.

93. Why do we choose our pathways?

Our pathways are set for our maximum achievement. I very often find that people with very difficult childhoods are the people who end up with the pathways of helping others because they have learnt from the difficulties within their own lives. Having difficult pathways also teaches us to have a non-judgemental view of others, and how to strive not to condemn others for what we have not experienced for ourselves. The North American Indians have a wonderful saying for this: "Do not judge another man until you have walked in his moccasins because only then may you truly understand all the feelings of a situation".

94. Do we choose our parents?

Yes, we do choose our parents. Again it's very hard for some of us to comprehend that we put ourselves through hell with parents by our own doing, but we choose our parents because we have something to learn from them and they have something to learn from us.

95. Why is the world so discontented?

There are many theories as to why our world seems to be all upside down and in a state. Strangely enough they are all very similar. The main thing that runs through all the theories is that our planet is changing alignment with all the other planets of our solar system. This means that great changes are taking place for all of us as our climate, our atmosphere, and our way of living will all be affected by these changes. At the moment our world does not quite know how to cope with what the human race has done to it, so volcanoes rumble, seas rise and winds are gale force. No one race or creed has supremacy anymore so no one knows who else to look to for help, or to sort out our wars and our differences – consequently there is great confusion all around us. The big changes are reputed to start happening approximately 2008–2012.

96. Why are a lot of people interested in Spirit these days?

People now need more and are searching for answers. Gone are the days where we just sit and believe that everything that we are told is the truth and that others can have a hand in our lives. We are starting to believe that we have to take responsibility for our own lives and that because we are not judged by God or Spirit we have to look into our hearts to see for ourselves what is right and wrong. Understanding and being a part of Spirit give us new understanding, new knowledge and most of all new freedom to think and to feel.

97. Why do we have to have darkness?

We have darkness for balance. As there is negative and positive there has to be a dark as well as a light. I do understand however that when the changes take place in our earth that darkness as it is now will be eradicated to a great extent. It will never go completely because of "balance" but it will be much more controllable than it is at the moment.

98. Why is there so much negativity at this moment?

At the moment there are an awful lot of people who are trying to bring the positivity/light to earth. This means that the negativity/darkness is fighting back. Each and every one of us has a part of our makeup that can work for the light or for the darkness, sometimes without even recognising which one we are working for. So there are times when our negative side can take over without us being aware of it. We can all learn to work from our positive sides by clearing our own negativity.

99. What can we do to help clear the negativity?

We can learn to work from our positive sides. The only way of doing this is to clear as much of our own negativity as possible – then we learn to be non-judgemental of others and their situations, and this means that we bring more chances for others to see their life in a balanced way rather than trying to make their decisions for them because we think that we know better. The more people that are balanced and making balanced decisions the more positivity is put into the earth. Another important way of helping to clear negativity is to ask the God light for help in the clearing.

100. What do we have to do with all the changes?

We are all part of the changes that are going on right at this minute of our lives – whether we are aware of it or not, whether we have already come onto our pathways yet or not – we are all a part of it. All we are here for is to understand our own potential, our own abilities and our own lights and most of all be able to help others to understand theirs.

101. What is the theory of Atlantis?

Atlantis is a city that in legend existed around the time of 106–43 BC. In the legend the people that lived in Atlantis were spiritually aware and an advanced people. Their power source was a huge crystal which was fine until some of the Atlantisans became greedy and wanted more power than others, so the whole of Atlantis became unbalanced, the crystal became overpowered and this caused the destruction of Atlantis. The crystal of Atlantis is supposed to be under the Bermuda triangle. It is said that in the time of change on our earth, parts of our land will disappear under the sea and parts will rise from the sea. The legend of Atlantis is that the crystal will rise and bring its energy with it but we must be ready to use it properly. I must stress that this is only one of the theories that float around and I just thought that readers might like to share it as it's my favourite.